St. Tammany Parish Postcards

Postcards

A Glimpse Back in Time

ST. TAMMANY PARISH POSTCARDS
A Glimpse Back in Time

by

Ashleigh Austin

PELICAN PUBLISHING COMPANY

Gretna 2005

*The word "Pelican" and the depiction of a pelican are trademarks
of Pelican Publishing Company, Inc., and are registered
in the U.S. Patent and Trademark Office.*

Library of Congress Cataloging-in-Publication Data

Austin, Ashleigh.
  St. Tammany Parish postcards : a glimpse back in time / by Ashleigh Austin.
    p. cm.
  ISBN 9781589802476 (alk. paper)
  1. Saint Tammany Parish (La.)–History–Pictorial works. 2. Saint Tammany Parish
(La.)–History, Local–Pictorial works. 3. Postcards–Louisiana–Saint Tammany Parish.
I. Title: Saint Tammany Parish postcards. II. Title.
  F377.S3A97 2005
  976.3'12'00222–dc22

                      2004025281

Printed in Singapore

Published by Pelican Publishing Company, Inc.
1000 Burmaster Street, Gretna, Louisiana 70053

CONTENTS

ACKNOWLEDGMENTS

I want to first thank Dr. Milburn Calhoun, my publisher, for giving me the opportunity to do this book; and I want to thank my editor, Nina Kooij, editor in chief, and Jim Calhoun, special projects editor, as well as the entire staff at Pelican for their help and support. Thank you, Robert Ewing III of Monroe, Louisiana, a fellow postcard-collector friend, who was the first to suggest I pursue a book project using my postcard collection.

Special thanks to the following people who gave me permission to publish their postcards in my collection: Bernard F. Holmes, photographer/publisher, Picture Postcards, Baton Rouge; Lynne Robertson Parker, president of Grant L. Robertson, Inc., Metairie, Louisiana; Ed Randazza, President of Express Publishing Co., Inc., New Orleans; Ron Giordano, CEO, H.S. Crocker, Co., Inc., Huntley, Illinois; and Debra Gust, Lake County Discovery Museum/Curt Teich Postcard Archives, Wauconda, Illinois. Special thanks to Charles J. Fritchie, Jr., curator of GOSH (Guardians of Slidell History) Museum, Slidell, Louisiana, for graciously helping to identify so many of the old places.

Special thanks to all those who helped with the research: Malise Prieto, clerk of court, St. Tammany Parish; Robin C. Leckbee, archivist, clerk of court, St. Tammany Parish; Janice L. Butler, director, St. Tammany Parish Library; Al Barron, Research Department, Covington Branch, St. Tammany Parish Library; Bill Larsen-Ruffin, Research Department, Slidell Branch, St. Tammany Parish Library; my sister, as well as my special friends, Lynn and Sherry, for being my "Louisiana legs" when I could not be there; and James M. Branum of Chattanooga, Tennessee, for helping to locate a former publishing company. Special thanks to William E. Stoner, attorney of Springfield, Missouri, for his guidance and support; and Gerry L. Averett of Gerry Averett Photography, Springfield, Missouri, for his photographic contributions.

I want to lovingly thank all my family and friends for their encouragement and support, especially my sons, daughter-in-law, and my sweet grandsons who are avid readers and cannot wait to see their Grammie's book in a bookstore! Last, but most importantly, I want to thank my wonderful husband for his constant love and endless support in everything I do, and for being my "Guy Friday" helping in ways too numerous to mention and for always being my biggest fan.

INTRODUCTION

My collection of old postcards began a few years ago, not as a hobby, but rather for my own personal reference as documentation of places that had either changed through the years, or no longer existed. Since photographs were not as plentiful in earlier years, I found that old picture postcards contained a wealth of information. I am so grateful to all those early postcard photographers and publishers for having the foresight to capture pieces of history that might not have been preserved any other way.

Being a photography buff much of my life, I found myself collecting more and more postcards of South Louisiana as my fascination with the pictorial history continued to unfold. As a result, I collected postcards far beyond the boundaries I had originally set for myself. In the process, I also learned that postcard era and stamp box dating, as well as the actual Curt Teich postcard dating system, played a major part in identifying the actual period the photos were taken. Many times, the personal messages written on the backsides not only carried additional information that helped to validate the times and places, but also provided priceless comments.

Surprisingly, the front photo alone was often incomplete without the additional information gleaned from those little details the average person would normally overlook. That was especially true of the postcards of the early 1900s.

That people today are visiting and relocating to St. Tammany Parish for very much the same reasons as the earliest settlers is evident in viewing these old postcards. I found it interesting and fitting that before World War II, the parish was referred to as the "Pink Parish" because of its abundance of pink tung oil tree blossoms. St. Tammany's beauty, along with her hospitality and country charm, is still very much alive. It is the fastest-growing parish in Louisiana.

I hope you will enjoy this pictorial history of St. Tammany Parish presented through old postcards dating back to the early 1900s. The journey takes us across Lake Pontchartrain from New Orleans, northeast to Slidell, with a loop around the lake through a number of cities before returning, via the causeway, to New Orleans.

St. Tammany Parish Postcards

A Glimpse Back in Time

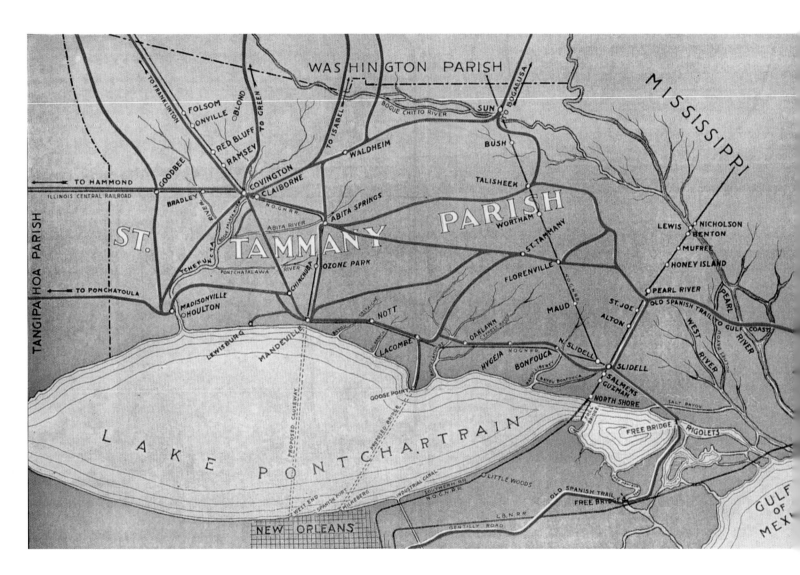

Chapter 1

NEW ORLEANS EAST TO ST. TAMMANY PARISH

Moonlight on Lake Pontchartrain, New Orleans, La. (J. Scordill, Three Stores, 505, 701 and 902 Canal St., New Orleans, La., 1907-1914). Author's note: Across Lake Pontchartrain from New Orleans is St. Tammany Parish, which comprises almost the entire northern shore of the lake.

MOONLIGHT ON LAKE PONCHARTRAIN, NEW ORLEANS, LA.

Chef Menteur Road, New Orleans, La. (C.B. Mason, New Orleans, La., 1915-1929). Author's note: This beautiful drive out in the country just outside New Orleans was the eastern route to St. Tammany Parish and to the Mississippi Gulf Coast prior to the opening in 1928 of the Pontchartrain Bridge, a toll bridge crossing eastern Lake Pontchartrain, and the later openings of the free Chef Menteur and Rigolets bridges.

CHEF MENTEUR ROAD, NEW ORLEANS, LA.

15

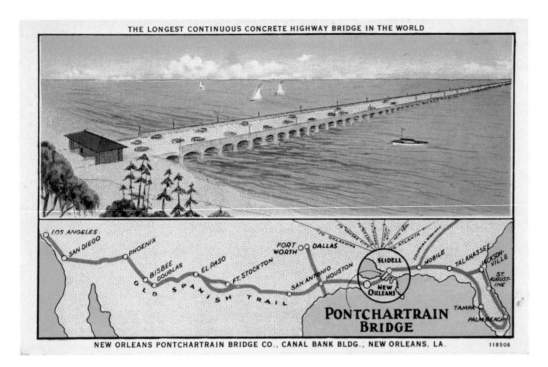

THE LONGEST CONTINUOUS CONCRETE HIGHWAY BRIDGE IN THE WORLD

PONTCHARTRAIN BRIDGE

NEW ORLEANS PONTCHARTRAIN BRIDGE CO., CANAL BANK BLDG., NEW ORLEANS, LA. 118506

The Longest Concrete Highway Bridge in the World. New Orleans Pontchartrain Bridge Co., Canal Bank Bldg., New Orleans, La. I have just crossed the longest concrete highway bridge in the world, just like riding on a smooth, paved and well lighted boulevard, with gas and repair service; telephones and even courteous traffic cops. Come to New Orleans this way. No ferries and it's the shortest route. (Alphonse Goldsmith, New Orleans, La., 1915-1929). Author's note: This was an advertisement postcard for the new Pontchartrain Bridge, a toll bridge that opened in 1928, and was the first bridge across Lake Pontchartrain, connecting New Orleans to St. Tammany Parish near Slidell. Its name would change several times, first from the Pontchartrain Bridge to the Watson—Williams Bridge, named after Eli Tullis Watson and George Elliot Williams whose investment firm was responsible for its financing. It was also called the Maestri Bridge after Mayor Bob Maestri of New Orleans, a supporter of Huey Long who opposed toll bridges. It became a free state bridge in 1938. The locals refer to it as the Five-Mile Bridge.

459   VIEW OF PONTCHARTRAIN BRIDGE, NEAR SLIDELL, LOUISIANA

View of Pontchartrain Bridge, Near Slidell, Louisiana. (Walhaven Brothers, Inc., Dallas, Texas, 1915-1929). Postmark: May 4, 1929.

Entrance to Pontchartrain Toll Bridge, Over Lake Pontchartrain, Near Slidell, Louisiana. (Walhaven Brothers, Inc., Dallas, Texas, 1915-1929)

458   ENTRANCE TO PONTCHARTRAIN TOLL BRIDGE, OVER LAKE PONTCHARTRAIN, NEAR SLIDELL, LOUISIANA

Pontchartrain Bridge, 5 Miles over Water, New Orleans, La. A fine example of modern progress in New Orleans is the demonstration of what is being done to improve highway connections in this part of the country. Looking north over the new $5,500,000 Pontchartrain Bridge, spanning Lake Pontchartrain from Point Aux Herbes, south of New Orleans, to Slidell on the north shore. The bridge, with its approaches, is the longest of its kind in the country. The actual span, entirely of concrete, is more than 5 miles in length and offers a chance for a beautiful cool drive over the waters of Lake Pontchartrain. It brings New Orleans subsequently closer to the North and East. (E.C. Kropp Co., Milwaukee, 1915-1929)

PONTCHARTRAIN BRIDGE, 5 MILES OVER WATER, NEW ORLEANS, LA.—147

Bridge across Lake Pontchartrain, New Orleans, La.
World's Longest Continuous Concrete Highway Bridge

Bridge across Lake Pontchartrain, New Orleans, La. World's Longest Continuous Concrete Highway Bridge. The bridge across Lake Pontchartrain, entering New Orleans on the Old Spanish Trail from the East. It is five miles long and cost $5,500,000. (Curt Teich, Chicago 1937)

Lake Pontchartrain Bridge, New Orleans, Louisiana

Lake Pontchartrain Bridge, New Orleans, Louisiana. The bridge across Lake Pontchartrain entering New Orleans, on Old Spanish Trail from the East. It is five miles long and cost $5,500.000. (Curt Teich, Chicago 1957). Author's note: This bridge was quite an accomplishment for Louisiana, as the Old Spanish Trail crossed the United States, from Florida, along the Gulf Coast, through the southwestern states, to Los Angeles.

Fort Pike and Rigolets Bridge, New Orleans, La. Fort Pike built in 1819. Fort Pike—One of the numerous forts in the vicinity of New Orleans is located on the Old Spanish Trail (U.S. 90). The land was reserved for military purposes under executive order dated February 9, 1842. Recently restored and beautified and converted into a state park. In the background is the toll-free span over the Rigolets, noted fishing resort, which connects Lake Borgne and Lake Pontchartrain. Although located about 35 miles from Canal Street, Rigolets is within the corporate limits of the City of New Orleans. (Curt Teich, Chicago 1937)

FORT PIKE AND RIGOLETS BRIDGE, NEW ORLEANS, LA.

Fort Pike, 30 miles east of New Orleans on Hwy. 90. Built at immense cost in 1838, as protection for New Orleans, Fort Pike never came under attack. The magnificence of craftsmanship is easily seen in its groin-vault chambers reached through barrel-vault corridors. It is presently open as a state park and provides an intriguing and delightful spot from which to view the Rigolets and waterways connecting Lake Pontchartrain and the Gulf of Mexico. Picnicking is allowed. **Color photo by Hubert A. Lowman.** (Grant L. Robertson— Box 8042 New Orleans, La., 1945-present). Author's note: The Rigolets Bridge connecting Orleans Parish with St. Tammany Parish can be seen in the distance.

BRIDGE OVER THE RIGOLETS, LA.
LOUISVILLE & NASHVILLE R. R.

Bridge Over the Rigolets, La. Louisville & Nashville R.R. Louisville & Nashville R.R. Souvenir (1907-1914). Author's note: The L&N Railroad grew into one of the country's major rail lines. By the 1880s, the trestle crossing the Rigolets and the southeastern tip of St. Tammany Parish connected the railroad from New Orleans to the Gulf Coast and Mobile.

Salmen Brick & Lumber Co., Slidell, La.
(H. G. Zimmerman & Co., Chicago, 1907-
1914). Postmark: May 25, 1910, A.M.,
Slidell, La. Received postmark: May 27,
1910, P.M., Lincoln, Neb. Author's note:
Fritz Salmen, arriving in the mid-1880s,
was one of Slidell's earliest builders. His
brickyard, Salmen Brick Works, was established between the railroad tracks and
Bayou Bonfouca, followed in the 1890s by
the Salmen sawmill, which became known
as the Salmen Brick and Lumber
Company. Salmen's brick yard supplied
bricks for building what would come to be
many of New Orleans' famous historic
buildings and hotels. In 1895, it supplied
one million bricks for the new St. Charles
Hotel. Other buildings included Maison
Blanche, D. H. Holmes, Hotel DeSoto, the
Grunewald Hotel, later known as the
Roosevelt Hotel, and many more.

Slidell Store Co., Slidell, La. (H. G.
Zimmerman & Co., Chicago, 1907-1914).
Postmark: April 14, 1909. Author's note:
Built and owned in the early 1880s by Fritz
Salmen, the Slidell Store Co. was also the
Salmen Commissary for the workers at the
Salmen Brick and Lumber Company. The
building still stands today at the corner of
Front Street and Cleveland Avenue.

Bank of Slidell, Slidell, La.

Bank of Slidell, Slidell, La. (H. G. Zimmerman & Co., Chicago, 1907-1914). Author's note: Located at the corner of Front and Cousin streets, the Bank of Slidell opened in December 1903 as an extension of the Covington Bank and in 1906 branched out on its own.

HIGH SCHOOL
SLIDELL, LA.

High School, Slidell, La. (1907-1914). Postmark: 1918. Author's note: Built at Carey and Brakefield streets in 1910, Slidell High was the first accredited high school in St. Tammany Parish.

(1910—1930 AZO Stamp Box). Author's note: This postcard shows several buildings on Front Street in Slidell. The large building is the Commercial Hotel that records of the GOSH (Guardians of Slidell History) Museum show the Salmen Brick and Lumber Company owning in 1929. Mrs. S.H. Lott was manager at that time. The building directly to the left of the Commercial Hotel is the early Neuhauser building that was owned by brothers U.G. and A.S. Neuhauser. The building farthest left is the Baker Hotel that was owned by C.L. Baker.

N.O. & N.E. Passenger Station, Slidell, La. (J.J. Dubisson, Slidell, La., 1907-1914). Author's note: This is the New Orleans and North Eastern Railroad Station, later the Slidell Depot, located on Front Street. Slidell's growth in the mid-1800s is attributed to the coming of the railroad. The building to the right shows a "Raleigh Rye" sign above the entry.

(1904—1920 CYKO Stamp Box). Author's note: This is the First Presbyterian Church, where services began in 1905. The old buggy-type cars seen at the lower left predate the Model-T, dating this postcard in the early 1910s.

M.E. Church, Slidell, La. (J.J. Dubisson, Slidell, La., 1907-1914). Author's note: This is the Methodist Episcopal Church.

Baptist Church, Slidell, La. (J.J. Dubisson, Slidell, La., 1907-1914). Author's note: The Slidell Baptist Church was located at Carey and Robert streets until 1974 when it was destroyed by fire.

High School, Slidell, La. (Curt Teich, Chicago 1932). Author's note: This new Slidell High School building was completed in 1924 on Third Street between Main Avenue and Pennsylvania Avenue. High school students attended classes here until 1961 when the present high school was built on Tiger Drive off Robert Road. L.V. McGinty, Sr. was principal at Slidell High School for over forty years until he retired in 1976.

White Kitchen. The South's Most Famous Highway Restaurants. Finest Foods, Expert Mixologists, Famous White Kitchen Sauce, 24-Hour Service since 1926, Modern Rest Rooms, 35 Miles East of New Orleans on U.S. Highway 11 and 190, Slidell, La. (H.S. Crocker, Co., Inc., San Francisco 1, California, 1945-present). Author's note: The cars date this postcard in the late 1940s to early 1950s. This White Kitchen restaurant, one of three built by Onesime Faciane, had been a well-known landmark restaurant for thirty-six years when it was destroyed by fire in October 1962. George Allen Bowden, a White Kitchen chef, made the famous barbeque sauce recipe. The White Kitchen was frequented not only by locals but also by New Orleanians and people traveling through Slidell from all directions. Without a doubt, everyone familiar with Slidell also knew of the White Kitchen with its Indian campfire sign, Southern hospitality, and good food.

White Kitchen. The South's Most Famous Highway Restaurants. Finest Foods, Expert Mixologists, Famous White Kitchen Sauce, 24—Hour Service since 1926, Modern Rest Rooms, 35 Miles East of New Orleans on La.—Miss. Short-Cut Highway U.S. 90. (H.S. Crocker Co., Inc., San Francisco 1, California, 1945-present). Postmark: October 10, 1954. Author's note: This White Kitchen restaurant was built in 1933 at the same time Onesime Faciane built the smaller White Kitchen restaurant on South Claiborne at Poydras Street in New Orleans. It was a favorite stopping place for those traveling U.S. 90 to and from the Gulf Coast. The cars date this postcard from the late 1940s to early 1950s.

Bosco's Restaurant, Motel and Lounge, 3599 Pontchartrain Road—Slidell, La.—Tel. 475. U.S. Hwy 11. Slidell's finest restaurant, most modern motel and lounge. Located in the heart of the famed Ozone Belt near the shores of beautiful Lake Pontchartrain. Bosco's features Fresh Gulf Seafoods, French, Italian and Northern Cuisine. (Curt Teich, Chicago 1963). Author's note: Bosco's, owned and operated by Sam Bosco, was another landmark restaurant in Slidell. As one can see by the signs in the foreground, it was more than a restaurant and lounge for the locals—it was their regular meeting place.

Cousin St., Slidell, La. One of the main thoroughfares of the older section of town, Cousin Street was once the heart of the business district. Here we see Haas Variety Store which has been a landmark in Slidell for many years. (Post Card Specialties 2629 Miss. Ave., Metairie, Louisiana, 1945-present). Author's note: The cars date this postcard in the late 1950s. Farther down the street is the Jitney Jungle grocery store, with the George Hotel above it, and Giordano's Shoe Store in the white building on the corner across the street. In the foreground is the old Polk Building. This area of Slidell is now known as "Olde Town," where many old buildings have been converted into night-clubs, antique and gift shops, restaurants, tea rooms, diners, and other places of entertainment.

Fontainebleau Hotel Court, Slidell, La.

Fontainebleau Hotel Court. Junction Highways 11 and 90 Slidell, La.— Telephone 643-2560. 30 modern units, air conditioning, telephone and T.V. in all rooms. Modern Restaurant, service station and lounge. Spacious Hotel Court grounds and ample parking. Located in the famed Ozone belt of La. Nearby is Beautiful Lake Pontchartrain and fabulous fishing. (Curt Teich, Chicago 1963). Author's note: This was one of Slidell's early motels whose location was very visible to passersby at the intersection of two major highways. The old red and blue U.S. MAIL box and Bell Telephone sign are visible in the foreground.

Holiday Inn, Slidell, Louisiana. I-10 & Gause Road (70458). 504/643-9770. (New Orleans 20 Mi.). Private Pool—Free Color TV—Individual A/C/ Units—Dining Room-Lounge—Free Advance Reservations. (1945-present). Author's note: The Holiday Inn was the first national chain motel built in Slidell. The cars date this postcard in the late 1950s to early 1960s.

Credit photo: Postcard of former Holiday Inn—Slidell appears courtesy InterContinental Hotels Group

The NASA Michoud Computer Operations' Computer Operations Office, located in Slidell, La., is one of the largest high-speed electronic computer centers in the country. The Office's analog and digital computers, operated for the National Aeronautics and Space Administration by Tele-computing Services, Inc., are divided into two basic complexes: A scientific data processing complex to perform engineering calculations arising in the development, fabrication and testing of the Saturn 1, Saturn 1B and Saturn V first stages being built at the main Michoud facility in New Orleans; and a management data complex to process such administrative information as payrolls and personal records. The Computer Office was established in July, 1962. (Curt Teich, Chicago 1965). Author's note: NASA brought with it a new population boom to Slidell. Slidell is the largest city in St. Tammany Parish.

The NASA Michoud Computer Operations, Slidell, La.

"Tranquillity," Slidell, La. Situated on beautiful Bayou Liberty, this typical early nineteenth century home was built on an original land grant in 1803 by Francais Du Buisson. The property was later acquired by Terence Cousin, who in 1840 erected the present main house around the pioneer structure. Cousin was the uncle of L'Abbe Adrien Rouquette, the renowned poet-priest "Chahta Ima," who served as missionary among the Choctaw Indians of St. Tammany Parish. (Curt Teich, Chicago 1968)

Chapter 3

OAKLAWN / LACOMBE

Oaklawn Inn. In the Ozone Belt—On N. O. Great Northern R. R. A "Piney Woods" Resort Without a Peer. One Year Round— No Consumptives Taken. Terms $8 to $10 per Week-Rates to Families. Hot and Cold Baths. Long Distance Phone. Mrs. G. C. Lafaye, Oaklawn, La. (1907-1914). Author's note: The resort, also a depot for guests, was on Bayou Lacombe where the N.O.G.N.R.R. trestle crossed the bayou. The inn boasted of being a resort "Without a Peer" in an attempt to encourage travel to the north shore of Lake Pontchartrain by train rather than by boat. Oaklawn is located on Highway 190 on the eastern outskirts of Lacombe.

IN THE OZONE BELT- ON N. O. GREAT NORTHERN R. R.

A "Piney Woods" Resort Without a Peer.

ONE YEAR ROUND   .'.   NO COMSUMPTIVES TAKEN

Terms $8 to $10 per Week - Rates to Families

Hot and Cold Baths.

Long Distance Phone.

MRS. G. C. LAFAYE,

Oaklawn, La.

Historic Bayou Lacombe. Bayou Gardens, Lacombe, La. Bayou Gardens, on the banks of historic Bayou Lacombe, creates a panorama of beauty that only Mother Nature can paint. Here where Chahta-Ima worked among the Choctaw Indians, the natural Charm and Beauty of the Bayou Country are preserved and enhanced by profuse planting of Camellias, azaleas, and other shrubs. The loveliness that pervades the atmosphere of this paradise of Louisiana cannot be put into words. (Curt Teich 1950). Author's note: Bayou Gardens was owned and developed as in the early 1950s by former Gov. Richard W. Leche. It became Holy Redeemer College in the mid-1950s when the property was sold to the Redemptorist order. The gardens presently surround the Southeastern Louisiana Refuges administrative offices and visitor center, located on Highway 434 off Highway 190 in Lacombe.

Historic Bayou Lacombe
Bayou Gardens, Lacombe, La.

Lourdes Shrine—Lacombe, La. The first Mass and consecration of Lourdes Shrine were on June 10, 1923 by Father Francois Balay, O.S.B. A beautiful spring-fed fountain flows near the Altar. Color by B. F. Holmes. (Bernard F. Holmes, Box 475, Baton Rouge, La., 1945-present). Author's note: Lourdes Shrine is nestled in a beautiful forest glen on Fish Hatchery Road in Lacombe.

Chapter 4

MANDEVILLE

Virgin Pines along U.S. Highway 190, near Covington, La. (Curt Teich, Chicago 1946). Author's note: This is actually at the entrance to Fontainebleau State Park on U.S. Highway 190 near Mandeville. The park is located between Lacombe and Mandeville.

Virgin Pines along U. S. Highway 190, near Covington, La.

6B344-N

Fontainebleau State Park Entrance near Covington, La. (Curt Teich, Chicago 1946). Author's note: Fontainebleau State Park is located near Mandeville.

Fontainebleau State Park Entrance near Covington, La.

6B342-H

33

Avenue of Oaks, Fontainebleau State Park, Mandeville, La.

Avenue of Oaks, Fontainebleau State Park, Mandeville, La. (Curt Teich, Chicago 1946). Postmark: Aug. 7, 1953. Author's note: This postcard was published the same year as the two previous ones, and the correct Mandeville location is shown.

Bath House and Concession Buildings, Fontainebleau State Park, Mandeville, La.

Bath House and Concession Buildings, Fontainebleau State Park, Mandeville, La. (Curt Teich, Chicago 1945). Author's note: The shore of Lake Pontchartrain lies just beyond these buildings.

Fontainebleau State Park, Mandeville, La. These are the remains of a sugar mill which once was part of a plantation owned by Bernard Xavier de Marigny de Mandeville, founder of Mandeville in 1830. This park offers complete camping facilities for year round camping. Located 3 miles East of Mandeville on Hwy. 190, it also features pool and lake swimming, hiking, picnicking and other activities. (Post Card Specialties, Metairie, New Orleans, La. 70003, 1945-present)

Drug Store and Post Office, Mandeville, La. (1907-1914). Postmark: 1912.

Lake Shore Front of Mugnier House, Mandeville, La.

Lake Shore Front of Mugnier House, Mandeville, La. (W.J. Tucker, Mandeville, La., 1907-1914). Postmark: Aug. 10, 1907. Author's note: The Mugnier House was located on Lakeshore Drive and later became the St. Tammany Hotel. This was one of many hotels built in Mandeville, as well as in Abita Springs and Covington, in the late nineteenth century to accommodate the influx of people who were drawn to the area as a result of the pure air of the Ozone Belt and the belief in the medicinal effects of the spring waters. Early steamboats, the most famous being the *New Camelia*, carried travelers on regular schedules across the lake from New Orleans. By 1880, Mandeville had the largest population in the parish.

Mugnier Hotel.

Mugnier Hotel. (Baker & Depre, Mandeville, La., 1907-1914). Author's note: This is another view of the Mugnier House above, named for the Mugnier brothers, A.G. and H. Mugnier, early businessmen in Mandeville who operated the Marquis G.P. de Marigny's Crescent Hotel and Restaurant in the late 1880s.

Mugnier Hotel Bath House and Pier, Mandeville, La. (W.J. Tucker, Mandeville, La., 1907-1914). Postmark: Aug. 10, 1907.

Mugnier Hotel Bath House and Pier, Mandeville, La.

Lake Boulevard, Mandeville, La. (L.A. Stockton's Pharmacy, Mandeville, La., 1907-1914). Author's note: Lake Boulevard, later named Lakeshore Drive, was lined with beautiful homes as well as fine restaurants and hotels with a breathtaking view of Lake Pontchartrain.

LAKE BOULEVARD   MANDEVILLE, LA.

GROUP OF RESIDENCES ON LAKE BOULEVARD   MANDEVILLE, LA.

Group of Residences on Lake Boulevard, Mandeville, La. (L.A. Stockton's Pharmacy, Mandeville, La., 1907-1914). Author's note: The Audubon Hotel with its white columns can be seen in the distance.

PUBLIC SCHOOL   MANDEVILLE, LA.

Public School, Mandeville, La. (L.A. Stockton's Pharmacy, Mandeville, La., 1907-1914). Author's note: Built in 1917 on Lafitte Street between Livingston and Monroe streets, the classrooms, accommodating students up through the ninth grade, were on the first floor, with offices upstairs. Note the seesaws and the round water fountain in front. Wing additions were later added to both sides of the building, and it later became Mandeville High School in the 1920s.

Catholic Church, Mandeville, La. (Curt Teich, Chicago 1926). Author's note: This is the old Our Lady of the Lake Church building where Catholic worship was held until 1953 when the new brick church was dedicated. The church dates back to 1850.

CATHOLIC CHURCH, MANDEVILLE, LA.

62366

Lake Shore Drive, Mandeville, La. (Curt Teich, Chicago 1946). Author's note: Now with paved road and sidewalks, this street was formerly named Lake Boulevard.

Lake Shore Drive, Mandeville, La.

6B36-N

Lake Pontchartrain and Shoreline of Mandeville, Louisiana

Lake Pontchartrain and Shorelines of Mandeville, Louisiana. (Curt Teich, Chicago 1953). Backside personal note: "They are getting ready to put a highway across this lake at a cost of 30 millions, it is 26 miles across to New Orleans. It [will] save 30 miles between N.O. and the East section of state. . . ." Author's note: The writing errors notwithstanding, it is evident the sender is referring to the causeway, which would actually be 24 miles long and cost much more than 31 million dollars.

Hotel St. Tammany, Mandeville, La.

Hotel St. Tammany, Mandeville, La. (Curt Teich, Chicago 1925). Date stamped on back: May 16, 1949. Author's note: This was the former Mugnier Hotel.

Chapter 5

ABITA SPRINGS

The Famous "Abita Springs," near Covington, La. (Trouilly & Oplatek, 1907-1914). Postmark: Aug. 25, 1910. Author's note: The Abita Springs Pavilion was built above the spring in 1888. Dr. T.M.D. Davidson owned the property in 1867 and promoted the early Choctaw Indians' belief in the healing powers of the spring water.

THE FAMOUS "ABITA SPRINGS," NEAR COVINGTON, LA.

TROUILLY & OPLATEK

The Famous Abita Springs. (Heintz & Aubert Pharmacy, Abita Springs, La. Made in Germany. 1907-1914). Postmark: July 1910. Backside personal note: "This is a healthy place. This is the place we go to get our drinking water. It surely is cool over here. They had a nice 4th of July over here. . . ."

The Famous Abita Springs.

New Abita Springs Hotel, Abita Springs, La.

New Abita Springs Hotel, Abita Springs, La. (Grombach—Faisans Co., Ltd. of New Orleans, La. Made in Germany. (1907-1914). Postmark: July 1911.

New Abita Springs Hotel, Abita Springs, La.

New Abita Springs Hotel, Abita Springs, La. (Heintz & Aubert Pharmacy, Abita Springs, La. Made in Germany. 1907-1914). Backside personal note: "You just ought to see the children[;] they certainly are enjoying themselves[;] they are thirsty about every 5 minutes because you know they want to go over to the little spring (the one in front of the house) to pump the water. . . ."

Arrival of Train at Abita Springs, La. (1907-1914). Postmark: June 1914. Backside personal note: "Here for a ride[;] went to the spring and drank plenty fine water[;] very warm. Going back by motor car in few minutes. . . ."

Main Street, Abita Springs, La. (Curt Teich, Chicago 1929). Author's note: The Abita Springs Pavilion is located at the end of Main Street.

GRAMMAR SCHOOL, ABITA SPRINGS, LA.

5893-29

Grammar School, Abita Springs, La. (Curt Teich, Chicago 1929)

Morgan's Swimming Pool and Spa, Abita Springs, La.

Morgan's Swimming Pool and Spa, Abita Springs, La. Morgan's Swimming Pool. This swimming pool is nearly 400 x 150 feet, concrete sides and white sand bottom. Continuous flow of sulphur water from large artesian well. Located on Abita, Mandeville Highway, 1 square from depot, large picnic grounds, modern bath house, showers, etc. (E.C. Kropp, Milwaukee, 1915-1929). Author's note: This was part of the Morgan's health resort.

The Comfort Apartments, Abita Springs, La. Emile Aubert, Proprietor. Up-to-date furnished apartments by the day, week or month. Situated in the "Land of the Pines" at Abita Springs, La. (E.C. Kropp, Milwaukee, 1915-1929). Author's note: Emile Aubert, co-owner of a pharmacy (note his pharmacy published several of the preceding Abita Springs postcards), was an alderman in 1903.

THE COMFORT APARTMENTS, ABITA SPRINGS, LA.

EMILE AUBERT, PROPRIETOR

Chapter 6
COVINGTON

The Famous and Historic Bogue Falia, Covington, La. (The Albertype Co., Brooklyn, N.Y. for J.S. Claverie, 1901-1907). Postmark: Nov. 17, 1908. [Bogue Falia is sometimes spelled Bogue Falaya.]

THE FAMOUS AND HISTORIC BOGUE FALIA, COVINGTON, LA.

Tchefuncta Bridge, Covington, La. (Curt Teich, Chicago 1905-1920). Postmark: May 1916. Backside personal note: "Thurs night 8 pm just arrived safe and a very pleasant trip over by boat. I feel the difference in the atmosphere on reaching Mandeville. [Q]uite chilly, quite a contrast from today in the City. . . ." [Tchefuncta is sometimes spelled Tchefuncte.]

TCHEFUNCTA BRIDGE.
COVINGTON. LA.

GATHERING TURPENTINE IN THE PINE FOREST, COVINGTON, LA.

Gathering Turpentine in the Pine Forest, Covington, La. (The Albertype Co., Brooklyn, N.Y., for J.S. Claverie, 1901-1907). Author's note: With the abundance of longleaf pine trees in St. Tammany Parish, scraping the thick, sticky resin created quite an export business for making turpentine used in countless number of products.

LARGEST FLOWING WATER WELL IN LOUISIANA, FLOWING 400 GALLONS A MINUTE DRILLED BY MARTIN & RATLIFF FOR ST. TAMMANNY ICE & M'F'G. CO.

Largest Flowing Water Well in Louisiana. Flowing 400 Gallons a Minute. Drilled by Martin & Ratliff for St. Tammany Ice & Mfg. Co. (The Albertype Co., Booklyn, N.Y., 1907-1914). Author's note: The St. Tammany Ice & Mfg. Co. also had the first electric generator in Covington.

Steamer *Josie*" Approaching Covington, La. (1907-1914). Postmark: April 8, 1914. Author's note: The *Josie,* captained by W.T.G. Weaver, began transporting passengers across Lake Pontchartrain in 1908.

STEAMER 'JOSIE'' APPROACHING COVINGTON, LA.

Rustic Landing, Bogue Falaya River, Covington, La. (1915-1929). Postmark: 1922. Author's note: The steamer *Josie* is seen at the landing. There were two landings in Covington—the Columbia Street landing at the end of the main downtown street and the old landing at the end of Jahncke Street.

RUSTIC LANDING, BOGUE FALAYA RIVER, COVINGTON, LA.

Claiborne Hotel, Covington, La. (1907-1914). Author's note: The Claiborne Hotel, opened in1880 as the Claiborne Cottage and overlooking the Bogue Falaya River, was one of the best known hotel resorts until it was destroyed by fire in 1912.

Ozonia Rest Cure. Covington, La. (Tolson & Schonberg, 1907-1929). Postmark: Oct. 10, 1909. Backside personal note: "Dear Mother, Am set here for the day. Am not taking the 'Rest Cure'. However but think this would be a good place to do so. Dick wanted me to look the place over and see what kind of place it would be to spend the Winter. . . ." Mailed to New York City, N.Y.) Author's note: The very name of this place, Ozonia Rest Cure, said it all to visitors who traveled from all parts of the country to New Orleans, then crossed the lake by steamboat to St. Tammany Parish's health spots.

Sunshine Cottage, near Covington, La. (The Rotograph Co., N.Y. City. Printed in Germany, 1907-1909). Postmark: July 1909. Author's note: This is another typical cottage of the early 1900s that accommodated visitors to the area in much the same way as the bed and breakfasts of today.

Sunshine Cottage, near Covington, La.

The Oaks, Covington, La. (The Rotograph Co., N.Y. City. Printed in Germany, 1907-1914). Postmark: March 1908, Covington. Received postmark: March 6, 1908, Baton Rouge. Author's note: This was later expanded into a larger resort hotel that a Dr. Young used as his sanitarium beginning in 1913.

The Oaks, Covington, La.

Glen Cottage, Covington, La. S.W. Prague, Proprietor. (1907-1914). Postmark: April 22, 1917. Stamp on front and back reads: No Consumptives Taken. Author's note: The same Dr. Young who used The Oaks Hotel as a sanitarium bought Glen Cottage in 1916.

Entrance to Sulphur Springs, Covington, near New Orleans, La. Covington is a favorite health resort located between the Bogue Falia and Tchefuncta River, just above the Forks. The land contains numerous springs, whose curative powers were first discovered by the Indians. (Raphael Tuck & Sons Series No. 2560, "New Orleans, La." 1907-1914). Art Publishers to their Majesties the King and Queen. Photochromed in Saxony.

Sulphur Springs, Covington, La. Sulphur Springs comprises a tract of 330 acres just north of Covington, bordering on the beautiful and historic Bogue Falaya River. The land contains numerous springs, whose curative powers were first discovered by the Indians. (Raphael Tuck & Sons, "Oilette," "Louisiana" Postcard 2549, 1907-1914). Art Publishers to their Majesties the King and Queen. Printed in England. Postmark: April 1908.

(Curt Teich, Chicago 1908-1913). Postmark: April 1921. Author's note: As one can see from this card, if the people were not busy promoting the healthy spring water, they were creating all sorts of homemade medicines to sell. Mackie's Pine Oil, "Nature's Greatest Healing Agent" as it reads on the hood of the car, looks like it could take care of just about anything. As an antiseptic, disinfectant, deodorant, and germicidal agent, as well as a pain reliever, it contained No Poison! It claimed to be "A Pure Vegetable Oil made from St. Tammany Pine Trees in the 'Ozone Belt."

Motor Line Crossing Bogue Falaya, Covington, La. (1907-1914). Postmark: July 25, 1912. Backside Personal Note: "Dearest Friend, This is the motor car we took to go to Covington, went to the Convent[;] it is a beautiful place. . . ." Author's note: The motor car was an electric train similar to the electric train that ran from the steamboat landing in Mandeville up to Abita Springs and over to Covington as a means to transport visitors over land to their various north shore destinations.

St. Tam & N.O. Rys. & Ferry Co. Cars Crossing Bogue Falia River, Covington, La. (1907-1914). Author's note: This is the electric train line of the St. Tammany and New Orleans Railway and Ferry Co. whose office was in Mandeville. These electric train cars ran a line from the steamboat landing in Mandeville to Abita Springs and Covington. Prior to the electric train line, people had to use horses or horse and carriage to take them to their destinations once they reached the north shore by steamboat.

Main Street, Covington, La. (1907-1914).
Postmark: May 1, 1914.

Covington, La. Next Stop. (1907-1914). Postmark: Feb. 1908. Author's note: By 1887, the East Louisiana Railroad had been completed from New Orleans to Slidell, Lacombe, Mandeville, and Abita Springs. Covington residents were anxiously waiting for the big day when it would finally be completed to their town. It was completed in February 1888.

Train Arriving at Covington, La.

Photo only Copyrighted 1907 by Tolson & Schonberg.

COVINGTON RESTAURANT —

Train Arriving in Covington, La. Photo only copyrighted 1907 by Tolson & Schonberg. Made in Germany (1907-1914). Postmark: April 25, 1910. Author's note: Visible on the right side of the street are the Covington Restaurant, J. Gilbert, Proprietor; a saloon; and the Roubion House. On the left are a combined livery stable and funeral home followed by a combined hotel and restaurant.

59411   RAILROAD DEPOT, COVINGTON, LA.

Railroad Depot, Covington, La. (Curt Teich, Chicago 1922-1925)

Court House, Covington, La. (1907-1914). Postmark: July 2, 1913. Author's note: The first courthouse was built in Claiborne, a town on the east side of the Bogue Falaya. This is a corner view of the courthouse later built on Boston Street.

Court House, Covington, La. (1914-1929). Author's note: Front view of the courthouse on Boston Street.

COURT HOUSE, COVINGTON, LA.

Covington Bank and Trust Company, Covington, La. (1907-1914). Postmark: Aug. 25, 1915. Author's note: The Bank of Covington opened in 1899 and in 1903 changed its name to Covington Bank and Trust Company. The bank had branches in Slidell and Franklinton.

Southern Hotel, Covington, La. (Acme Book & News, Co., 1907-1914). Postmark: Dec. 20, 1912. Author's note: The Southern Hotel, located at the corner of Boston and New Hampshire streets, opened in 1907 at a cost of $100,000 with 200 feet of galleries, a formal garden, and a tennis court. The lobby surrounded an artesian fountain.

Covington High School, Covington, La.
(Curt Teich 1908-1913)

Covington High School, Covington, La.

Dixon Academy, Covington, La. Photo only copyrighted 1907. (Tolson & Schonberg, 1907-1914). Author's note: Dixon Academy, with Wm. A. Dixon as principal, was a private school that opened in October 1907 and later became St. Paul's Academy. Boasting a new $10,000 gymnasium with a large swimming pool, it was quite a school in its day.

Dixon Academy, Covington, La.

St. Paul's Academy. (1907-1914)

St. Scholastica's Convent, Covington, La. (The Valentine & Son's Publishing Co. Ltd., New York, 1907-1914). Printed in Great Britain.

St. Scholastica's Convent and Academy, Covington, La. (Curt Teich, Chicago 1924). Author's note: Established in 1903 and incorporated in 1907, St. Scholastica's Academy was a boarding and day school for girls operated by the Benedictine Sisters.

ST. SCHOLASTICA'S CONVENT AND ACADEMY, COVINGTON, LA.   120545

Pavilion at Park, Covington, La. (1907-1914). Postmark: Aug. 24, 1911. Backside personal note: "It was beautiful this morning but it rained this afternoon. It looks like I never will get that long walk in the woods. I am feeling very good—I weighed today[.] I gained five pounds. I sure do like this fine water. . . ."

Pavilion at Park, Covington, La.

Pavilion, Bogue Falaya Park,
Covington, La.

Pavilion, Bogue Falaya Park, Covington, La. (1907-1914). Author's note: This was a popular gathering place for all sorts of recreational activities and picnics.

(1907—1929 NOKO Stamp Box). Author's note: This downed tree just missed the Bogue Falaya Pavilion. This offers a closer view of the inside of the pavilion.

Pavilion, Bogue Falaya Park, Covington, La. (1907-1914)

Bridge over Bogue Falaya River, Covington, La. (1907-1914). Postmark: 1921.

BRIDGE OVER BOGUE FALAYA RIVER, COVINGTON, LA.

Entrance to Covington, La. over Bogue Falaya River Bridge

OA3981

Entrance to Covington, La., over Bogue Falaya River Bridge. (Curt Teich, Chicago 1930)

CHAROPIN PARK, COVINGTON, LA.

25-19

Charopin Park, Covington, La. (1907-1914). Backside personal note: "Here's a pretty spot in Covington. Just the place for a nice quiet boat ride for two. . . ." Author's note: Emile Charropin bought the Crystal Springs Hotel, a private boarding house, and property in 1902 from Rosa Gonthier and later sold it to Grasper Cusachs in 1920. An area land map shows a beach house and park at the foot of Lee Road on the Bogue Falaya River.

Charropin Beach, Covington, La. (Curt Teich, Chicago 1938). Postmark: 1938.

Charropin Beach, Covington, La.

Jim's Free Beach, Covington, La. (Curt Teich, Chicago 1938)

Jim's Free Beach, Covington, La.

Moss Covered Oaks, Jahncke Ave., Covington, La.

Moss Covered Oaks, Jahncke Ave., Covington, La. (Curt Teich, Chicago 1938). Author's note: This street, named after the family who donated shells for the road, is typical of the beautiful settings throughout the parish.

Highway Scene on Military Road, Covington, La.

Highway Scene on Military Road, Covington, La. (Curt Teich, Chicago 1940). Author's note: This was road used by Gen. Andrew Jackson on his way from Tennessee to fight the Battle of New Orleans. He then went by boat across Lake Pontchartrain to New Orleans. A military post established on the river north of Covington led to the name Military Road.

View of Waldheim Gardens—Covington, Louisiana. (Curt Teich, Chicago 1941). Author's note: The property was originally owned by Tulane University and later became the Jahncke property.

VIEW OF WALDHEIM GARDENS — COVINGTON, LOUISIANA   18107-N

St. Peter's Church, Covington, La. (Curt Teich, Chicago 1946). Author's note: St. Peter's was founded about 1843 and was served by Father Adrien Rouquette.

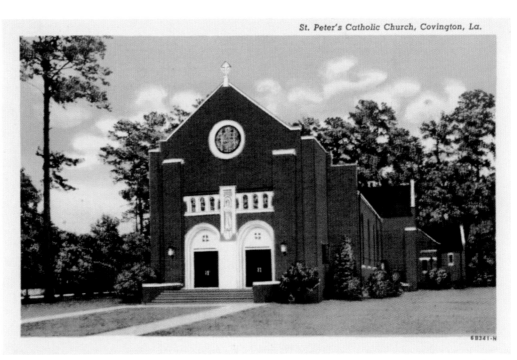

St. Peter's Catholic Church, Covington, La.

6B341-N

67

Covington High School, Covington, La.

Covington High School, Covington, La. (Curt Teich, Chicago 1946). Author's note: This was formerly the Lyon High School.

A Beautiful Drive in one of Covington's Estates, Covington, La.

A Beautiful Drive in one of Covington's Estates, Covington, La. (Curt Teich, Chicago 1940). Author's note: This estate on the Bogue Falaya River was owned by Sigmund Odenheimer of New Orleans who was prominent in the cotton manufacturing business as well as civic and industrial interests. In 1924, Odenheimer donated the aquarium and the sea lion pool, two major additions, to Audubon Park. His home in Covington was likely a weekend and summer residence.

Odenheimer Home, Covington, La. (Curt Teich, Chicago 1940)

Odenheimer Home, Covington, La.

OB434-N

Falls in the Odenheimer Estate, Covington, La. (Curt Teich 1940)

Falls in the Odenheimer Estate, Covington, La.

OB435-N

Pool and Fountain in Merritt Gardens, Covington, La.

6B340-N

Pool and Fountain in Merritt Gardens, Covington, La. (Curt Teich, Chicago 1946). Author's note: Another beautiful view of an estate in Covington.

Chapter 7

ST. BENEDICT

St. Joseph Abbey—St. Benedict, La. (1907-1914). Author's note: St. Joseph Abbey was founded in the early 1900s by the Benedictines, who acquired Cedar Hill, a plantation owned by James R. Hosmer, and also began St. Joseph College for boys.

ST. JOSEPH ABBEY — ST. BENEDICT, LA.

St. Joseph's Abbey Church, St. Benedict, La. (E.C. Kropp, Milwaukee, 1907-1914). Author's note: The abbey building is at the left.

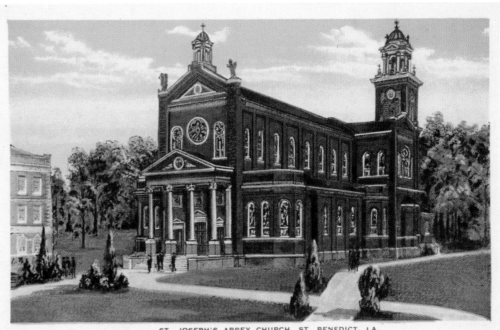

ST. JOSEPH'S ABBEY CHURCH, ST. BENEDICT, LA.

Chapter 8
GOODBEE

The Old Goodbee Ford, Near Covington, La. (Trouilly & Oplalek, 1907-1914). Postmark: Mar. 21, 1908. Author's note: Streams flowing southward across the Florida Parishes carried white sand and gravel, building many historic fords across them. As a result, early steamboats and schooners could navigate only the lower parts of the streams. The Tchefuncte was navigable only to Covington. However, the fords provided a means for horses and wagons to cross where there were no bridges.

Chapter 9

MADISONVILLE/ HOULTONVILLE

Road to Madisonville, from Covington, La. (Trouilly & Oplatek, 1907-1914). Postmark: Aug. 11, 1907.

In the "Pines" of "St. Tammany." Residence of W.L. Houlton, Houltonville, La. (Whitten & Dennison, West Bethel, Me., 1907-1914). Postmark: Jan. 31, 1910, Houltonville. Author's note: This house, built in the 1880s as the residence of William Theordore Jay, a sawmill owner, became the home of William L. Houlton, who later bought the lumber company from W.T. Jay. Houltonville was named after W.L. Houlton, and the home stills stands in Fairview—Riverside State Park. It is now the Otis House Museum, named after Frank Otis, who bought the house and renovated it as a summer home in the 1930s.

75

Chapter 10
CAUSEWAY TO NEW ORLEANS

Lake Pontchartrain Causeway, World's Longest Bridge. Lake Pontchartrain Causeway, the world's longest bridge (23.83 miles), connecting New Orleans with the highlands to the north. It was completed in 1956, at a cost of 51 million dollars, as part of the Greater New Orleans Expressway System. Eight miles of the bridge are out of sight of land. (Grant L. Robertson, Metairie, New Orleans, La., 1945-present). Author's note: It was the opening of this bridge to west St. Tammany Parish that spurred the growth in that area. The date of this postcard is the mid-1950s-early 1960s.

LAKE PONTCHARTRAIN CAUSEWAY, WORLD'S LONGEST BRIDGE

Lake Pontchartrain Toll Bridge, New Orleans, La. Through this toll gate you go across the world's longest bridge. It stretches for 24 miles across the wide waters of Lake Pontchartrain. (Express Publishing Co., Inc., Metairie, La., 1945-present). Author's note: The photograph on this postcard was taken in the mid-1950s-early 1960s.

LAKE PONTCHARTRAIN CAUSEWAY

Lake Pontchartrain Causeway. The longest bridge in the world stretches for 24 miles across the wide waters of Lake Pontchartrain near New Orleans. (Express Publishing Co., Inc. Metairie, La., 1945-present). Author's note: The photograph is from the mid-1950s-early 1960s.

Lake Pontchartrain Causeway. This 24-mile bridge, built at a cost of 51 million dollars, is the longest overwater highway bridge in the world. (Completed 1956). (Bernard F. Holmes, P.O. Box 475, Baton Rouge, La., 1945-present). Author's note: This is a view of the old "turnaround" placed near the middle of the bridge for those who might not want to travel its entire length. It has since been closed. The date of this postcard is the mid-1950s-early 1960s.

Lake Pontchartrain Causeway. Lake Pontchartrain Causeway, connecting Greater New Orleans with the highlands to the North. The World's longest highway bridge, 125,927 feet (23.83 miles) from shore to shore, it was completed in 1956 as part of the Greater New Orleans Expressway System, costing 51 million dollars. Eight miles of the bridge are out of sight of land. Curt Teich, Chicago 1957)

Lake Pontchartrain Causeway

Lake Pontchartrain Causeway, World's Longest Bridge. The world's longest bridge (23.83 miles), connecting New Orleans with the highlands to the north, is part of the Greater New Orleans Expressway System, and is considered to be one of the world's safest bridges. Eight miles of the bridge are out of sight of land. (Grant L. Robertson, Metairie, Louisiana 70001, 1945-present). Author's note: The second bridge span was built from 1967 to 1969 and opened in May 1969. The bridges are eighty feet apart and are connected by seven crossovers for motoring emergencies.

LAKE PONTCHARTRAIN CAUSEWAY, WORLD'S LONGEST BRIDGE

SOURCES

The following sources were most helpful in the preparation of this book:

Archives and Land Records, Clerk of Court, St. Tammany Parish.

Archives and Reference Department, St. Tammany Parish Library.

Inside Northside Magazine Online.

Mandeville on the Lake. A Sesquicentennial Album 1840-1990, C. Howard Nichols; St. Tammany Historical Society, Inc., Mandeville, Louisiana, 1990.

Mr. Kentzel's Covington 1878-1890, Carol Saunders Jahncke; Legacy Publishing Company, Inc., Baton Rouge, LA, 1979.

Notes on Slidell History, Charles J. Fritchie, Jr.; GOSH (Guardians of Slidell History), Slidell, LA 1999.

Slidell "Camellia City," Dan Ellis; Dan Ellis, Pass Christian, MS 1999.

St. Tammany Parish L'autre Cote du Lac, Frederick S. Ellis; Pelican Publishing Company, Inc., Gretna, LA, 1998.